Jeff Gordon

by Mark Stewart

PHOTO CREDITS
All photos courtesy AP/Wide World Photos, Inc. except the following:

David Taylor/Allsport – 5 top, 6, 21 bottom, 33
John Mahoney – 12, 13, 15, 16, 20 top. 20 bottom left, 28 bottom, 31 bottom, 36, 37, 46
J. D. Cuban/Allsport – 29, 39
Mark Stewart – 48

STAFF
Project Coordinator: John Sammis, Cronopio Publishing
Series Design: The Sloan Group
Design and Electronic Page Makeup: Jaffe Enterprises, and
        Digital Communications Services, Inc.

LIBRARY OF CONGRESS CATALOGING-IN-PUBLICATION DATA
Stewart, Mark.
    Jeff Gordon / by Mark Stewart
        p. cm. – (Grolier All-Pro Biographies biographies)
    Includes index.
    Summary: A brief biography of the youngest driver to win the Winston Cup title, which he did
in 1995 at the age of twenty-four.
    ISBN 0-516-20224-3 (lib. binding)–ISBN 0-516-26032-4 (pbk.)
    1. Gordon, Jeff, 1971-   –Juvenile literature. 2. Automobile racing drivers–United States–
Biography–Juvenile literature. [1. Gordon, Jeff, 1971-   . 2. Automobile racing drivers.] I. Title.
II. Series.
GV1032.G67S84 1996
796.7'2'092–dc20
[B]
                                                                                    96-20083
                                                                                    CIP
                                                                                    AC

Grolier **ALL-PRO** Biographies™

Jeff Gordon

by
Mark Stewart

CHILDREN'S PRESS®
A Division of Grolier Publishing
New York • London • Hong Kong • Sydney
Danbury, Connecticut

Contents

Meet

Jeff Gordon

He was out-driving teenagers when he was a little kid. He was out-maneuvering adults when he was a teenager. Today, he is out-foxing the most experienced drivers in the world as the brightest young talent on the stock-car racing scene. His name is Jeff Gordon, and this is his story . . .

Growing Up

When most people look at a green, grassy hillside, they think about its beauty. When three-year-old Jeff Gordon looked at the hill behind his house in Vallejo, California, he just wanted to roll down it as fast as he could. He spent many days running and rolling down the hill. He would smack into a tree, flop into a puddle, or go bouncing along on his bottom. Regardless of the bumps and bruises, Jeff just wanted to get back up that hill as fast as he could so he could come hurtling down it again.

Since the age of three, Jeff Gordon has loved anything with wheels.

When Jeff was five, he drove quarter-midget cars.

I rode my first bicycle when I was two and a half or three years old," Jeff says. "I remember those days. We had a big hill at our house, and I used to ride down that hill on my bike, skateboard, roller skates—whatever I had."

Anything with wheels was fascinating to Jeff. By the time he was four, he was entering BMX bicycle races and holding his own against older riders. Jeff's mother, Carol, was against the idea. She saw how many kids wound up in the emergency room after accidents. Jeff's stepfather, John Bickford, convinced his wife that Jeff might be safer driving a quarter-midget, a car about six feet long powered by a tiny, one-cylinder engine. Jeff thought it would be cool to drive a real car, but he was scared at first. Working the steering wheel, gas pedal, and brakes at the same time was difficult. But soon he got used to it, and he and his stepfather went out driving every chance they got.

eff soon entered his first official race. He was so nervous that he spun out at nearly every turn. The kids he was competing against were all much older than Jeff, and they laughed at the idea of a five-year-old competing on the same track as them. But within two years, there was nothing funny about racing against Jeff—he won 36 main events. And the following year, he won every race he entered at the two tracks near his home. Although Jeff was just eight years old, he was crowned the Grand National Champion at the year-end competition in Denver, Colorado.

Much of the credit for Jeff's stunning success went to his stepfather, who taught Jeff about practice, strategy, and maintenance. On the Jeff Gordon racing team, nothing was left to chance. When Jeff needed new equipment, his stepfather simply would sell the car in which Jeff had won his latest championship. Someone was always willing to buy a "winning" car. Jeff's mother also pitched in, often driving the truck and trailer to and from events when her two men were too exhausted to do anything other than fall asleep.

Jeff was nine when he decided to try driving go-karts, which have 10-horsepower engines. Competing against 15-, 16-, and 17-year-olds, Jeff entered 25 speedway events in

California and won every single race! Jeff moved up a class and continued to win, this time against adult drivers. They hated being beaten by a little kid, and they let him know it. Feeling unwelcomed—and unchallenged—on the go-kart circuit, he went back to racing quarter-midgets and won the Grand National Championship again.

By the time Jeff turned 13, he had won everything in sight. The next classification of racing was the sprint-car circuit. These cars were not 10- or 20-horsepower lightweights. They packed 600 horses and more under the hood. At first, Jeff believed he was too young to be allowed to drive one of these monsters. But then he heard about the All-Star Series, which had no minimum-age requirement in its rulebook. This organization did not figure any 13-year-old would be crazy enough to drive in its races, so it never made a rule against it. Jeff and his stepfather built a 1,300-pound, 650-horsepower vehicle at a cost of around $25,000, and Jeff began racing in the All-Star's winter circuit in Florida.

Jeff's family was convinced that he had a bright future in racing. They moved to Indiana so they could be in the heart of sprint-car country. He was now racing against some of the best drivers in America, and as usual, he was beating them. In fact,

Jeff won three races before he was old enough to obtain an Indiana driver's license!

While attending Tri-West High School, Jeff had to work very hard to keep up with his studies. Although he raced on the weekends and several nights a week, he got his homework done and rarely missed a day of school. Luckily, most of the events Jeff entered were close to his home in Pittsboro. When he had to travel and miss a few days of school, he would complete all of his assignments in advance. Jeff's favorite class was science. His teacher, Mr. Williams, was a big racing fan and a member of a local hot rod club. They would talk about the science involved in racing and how an engine works. They remain very good friends to this day.

You might think that a kid as successful as Jeff would act like a big shot in school. But that was not the case. In fact, Jeff was so low-key about his racing success that many students at Tri-West had no idea that he was the most famous young driver in the Midwest.

One of Jeff's first USAC starts was in this sprint car at Eldora Speedway.

The only time anyone really noticed him was when he and his friends attended school sporting events. Jeff would be in the front row, screaming his lungs out for the Bruins. By the time Jeff graduated, he was the most popular boy in his class, and was voted king of the senior prom.

"Regular guy" Jeff at seventeen

At 16, Jeff obtained his racing license from the United States Automobile Club (USAC), and after graduation, he began racing on the sprint-car circuit full-time. Between the ages of 16 and 20, he won 22 USAC races and had 55 top-five finishes, driving everything from midgets to championship dirt cars. When Jeff was 17, he traveled halfway around the world to race in New Zealand, where the "summer" racing season takes place from December through February. He won 14 of 15 races before coming back home. At age 19, Jeff drove his midget car to the USAC national championship. At 20, he was USAC's national dirt track champion, becoming the youngest driver ever to win the coveted Silver Crown. There was not much else for Jeff to win. His mother and stepfather agreed with him that it was time to take the final step in building his career.

The Road

In June 1990, 18-year-old Jeff Gordon climbed into the cockpit of a stock car for the first time in his life. He had enrolled in a driving school run by NASCAR legend Buck Baker to see if stock-car racing interested him. After just a few spins around the track at the Rockingham Motor Speedway in North Carolina, Jeff knew this was where he belonged. "That first day, the first day I got in a car," Jeff recalls. "I said, 'This is it. This is what I want to do.' The car was different from anything that I was used to. It was so big and heavy. It felt very fast, but very smooth. I loved it."

Making the jump to stock-car racing was unheard of at Jeff's age. Building and maintaining these vehicles is very expensive, and at first no investors or team owners were willing to gamble several hundred thousand dollars on a teenager, no matter how spectacular his record was. But as Jeff continued to capture headlines in other USAC races, it became harder to

Jeff (second from left) celebrates a phenomenal double win (sprint and midget) in 1990.

ignore the fact that he belonged in the big leagues.

Toward the end of the 1990 season, Jeff got sponsorship money from a chain of steakhouses and joined the Busch Grand National circuit. The Busch series is considered the final stepping stone to the NASCAR circuit, which represents the

In 1991, Jeff won the USAC Silver Crown Championship.

pinnacle of stock-car racing. In 1991, car owner Bill Davis gave Jeff his first full-time ride.

All eyes were on Jeff. He was the youngest driver on the track, and fans were anxious to see if he could carry his success at lower levels into the big time. At first, he was finishing races in the back of the pack. But as Jeff gained experience, he began to creep up on the leaders and finished as Busch Series Rookie of the Year and earned $111,608 in prize money. More important to his career, however, was that his relationship with crew chief Ray Evernham was starting to click. Evernham had been skeptical about working with such a young driver when he first met Jeff, but as they worked together they realized they could make a strong team.

"When we first started working together, Ray impressed me, and I guess I impressed him, " says Jeff. "He impressed me because he had been a race-car driver. A lot of crew chiefs have never driven a race car, but Ray knew exactly what the car was doing."

Jeff's dramatic success in just his second full year of stock-car racing earned him a shot at the Winston Cup circuit. In 1992, this "meeting of the minds" produced three wins and 15 Top Ten finishes. Jeff caught the eye of Ray Hendrick, who is one of the country's most successful car owners, and Hendrick asked him to join his team and step up to the Winston Cup circuit. It was a huge opportunity, but Jeff told Hendrick he wanted to remain loyal to his current owner, who was trying to raise the money to form a team of his own. Only when Bill Davis failed to secure the necessary sponsors, did Jeff sign with Hendrick. It was one of the most difficult decisions of his life.

Jeff's first Winston Cup appearance came at Atlanta, in the final race of the 1992 season. He cut a tire and dropped out of the race just before the midway point to finish a disappointing 31st. That same day, Richard Petty, the winningest driver in NASCAR history, ran his last race. No one knew it at the time, but the 1992 Hooters 500 would go down in auto-racing history as the ultimate "passing of the torch" from one legendary driver to another.

Ray Hendrick and his wife after Ray won the 1977 Talladega 300

Jeff Gordon's first race of the 1993 season was the 125-mile qualifier for the Daytona 500. It had been 30 years since a rookie had won the race, and no one expected Jeff to win his first time out. But that is just what he did. Jeff was so inexperienced that after taking the checkered flag, he had no idea where to find Victory Lane! Three days later, he finished a very respectable fifth at the Daytona 500. By year's end, Jeff had established himself as one of NASCAR's top drivers, and he easily won the Rookie of the Year award.

In 1994, Jeff won his first Winston Cup race, the Coca-Cola 600 in Charlotte, North Carolina. It was a hair-raising win over veterans Rusty Wallace and Ricky Rudd, and Jeff did not take the lead until there were eight laps to go. Overcome by his victory, he burst into tears in front of millions of television viewers after the race. Six weeks later, Jeff returned home to Indiana for the first running of the Brickyard 400. This race marked the first time stock cars would compete at the Indianapolis Motor Speedway, which until then had only hosted IndyCar competition. Jeff, who had

In 1993, Jeff won the Winston Cup rookie award and Dale Earnhardt (right) won the championship.

turned 23 just two days earlier, roared to victory by a half-second over Brett Bodine. The landmark win by the transplanted "hometown boy" touched off one of the wildest victory celebrations the state had ever seen. As for Jeff, he simply ordered a pizza and watched a tape of the race with his future wife, Brooke.

Jeff's big year was nothing compared to what would follow. In 1995, he won seven races, including four during a remarkable seven-week period. He led all drivers with more than $2 million in winnings and drove away with the

Jeff's performance in Atlanta ensured the 1995 Winston Cup championship.

Winston Cup title at the age of 24. To put this achievement in proper perspective, consider that of the ten drivers who won the championship before him, only one—27-year-old Richard Petty—did it before the age of 28. The average age of those drivers at the time of their ninth win was over 30!

"Winning the title is just too good to be true," said Jeff at the time. "There just aren't words to describe how I feel. It's been a spectacular year—better than we ever thought it could be."

Timeline

1991: Wins USAC Silver Crown championship

1993: Named Winston Cup Rookie of the Year

1990: Wins USAC Midget National Championship

1996: Jeff continues to dominate the Winston Cup circuit

1995: Takes Winston Cup title with seven victories

1994: Wins first Winston Cup race, Coca-Cola 600 at Charlotte

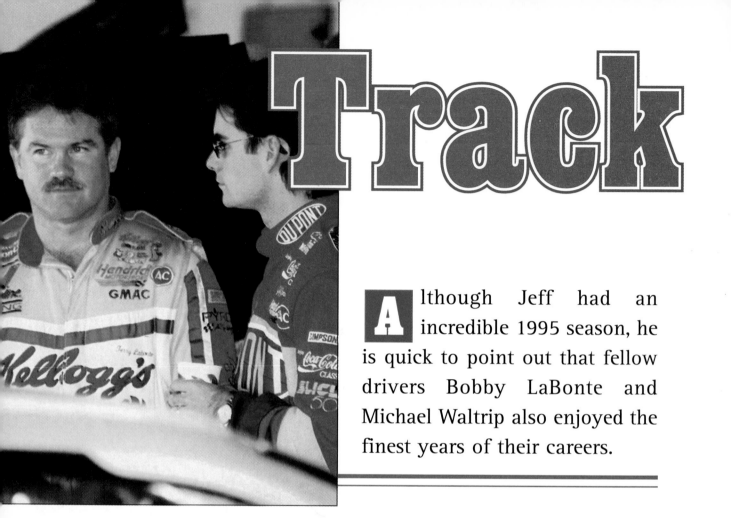

Track

Although Jeff had an incredible 1995 season, he is quick to point out that fellow drivers Bobby LaBonte and Michael Waltrip also enjoyed the finest years of their careers.

Drivers Terry LaBonte (left) and Jeff talk about their cars before the Daytona 500.

The first time team owner Rick Hendrick saw Jeff race, he was sure he was going to crash. Instead, Jeff won the race!

Jeff drives car number 24, a Chevrolet Monte Carlo. The brightly colored vehicle earned his crew one of racing's great nicknames: The Rainbow Warriors.

Action!

R equests for Jeff to do personal appearances have doubled since he won the Brickyard 400 in 1994, but he still tries to make as many as possible. "It's tough, but you've got to get out to the fans. That's important in our sport."

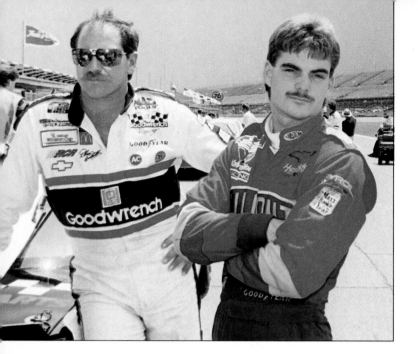

Dale Earnhardt (left) and Jeff discuss strategy before qualifying for the 1992 Daytona 500.

Jeff has been with crew chief Ray Evernham for his entire NASCAR career. "We wouldn't stick together if we didn't work well together and didn't respect each other."

There are a lot of NASCAR drivers who will play it safe and take the points for finishing fifth or sixth. Jeff refuses to hang back if he has a shot at winning a race.

After just two years on the Winston Cup circuit, Jeff was being compared to all-time greats Dale Earnhardt and Rusty Wallace.

Jeff has been likened to a young Richard Petty. "I'd like to think that someday, when people might think about me, they would say only one-hundredth of the nice things they say about Richard. . . . I don't think anyone can be another Richard Petty."

Jeff's ability to control an automobile astounds many racing insiders. Even the greatest drivers totaled a car or two when they were his age.

Jeff's landmark victory at the 1994 Brickyard 400—just a few miles from where he grew up—was his most emotional NASCAR victory. "That's why I took an extra lap. I wanted to wipe away the tears."

Pit crews frantically work on their cars during the 1994 Brickyard 400, which Jeff won.

Dealing

When Jeff Gordon was ready to join the Winston Cup circuit, it meant leaving Bill Davis, the sponsor who had given him his first real shot at stock-car racing. He knew that splitting with Davis would make him look ungrateful, but he realized that he had to move on.

"I've never had so much negative response to anything I've ever done. . . . It was a tough decision, and I didn't know how it was going to turn out. But I felt that I was making the best decision for Jeff Gordon."

Jeff celebrates victory with
an intentional spin after
crossing the finish line.

With It

How Does

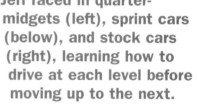

Jeff raced in quarter-midgets (left), sprint cars (below), and stock cars (right), learning how to drive at each level before moving up to the next.

He Do It?

Although it sometimes seems that way, Jeff Gordon was not born to be a stock-car driver. He worked his way up the racing ladder slowly and carefully. Jeff, his mother, and his stepfather agreed that he would not switch to a more powerful car—or move into a more competitive classification—until he had mastered the level where he was. The only reason Jeff joined NASCAR at such an early age was because he was able to prove himself so quickly at each stage of his career.

The Grind

Working your way up the auto-racing ladder from quarter-midgets to stock cars can be a long, hard journey. It means driving hundreds of miles every week from event to event, and learning how to fix your own car. The hours are long, the food is bad, and your bedroom often is a sleeping bag in the flatbed of a mud-spattered pickup truck. Most drivers experience these hardships in their early 20s. But Jeff Gordon started paying his dues when he was 13 years old. No wonder he could handle the challenges of NASCAR at such a young age!

"There's so much that goes on away from the track. You have to be prepared to do a lot of things if you're going to be successful."

Jeff has to be prepared to race in any kind of weather, including temperatures below freezing (top right). During USAC midget races, Jeff was his own pit crew (bottom right).

Family

Jeff and his fiancée Brooke Sealey celebrate a victory.

When Jeff Gordon accepted the winner's trophy at the 125-mile qualifying race at Daytona in 1993, he met Brooke Sealey in Victory Lane. The 21-year-old rookie and the beauty queen hit it off immediately, but drivers and Winston Cup models were not allowed to see each other socially. All year long, drivers and race officials wondered why Jeff never took a date to parties, and why Brooke did not have a boyfriend. At a party thrown by fellow driver Dale Earnhardt after the December NASCAR awards banquet, they decided to let the racing world in on a little secret. During the party, they danced the night away, and soon everyone realized that they

Matters

had been dating secretly all year long! They were married 11 months later and have been inseparable ever since.

"It's hard for me to have a lot of friends. . . . I work on the weekends and most other people my age work during the week. When they're hanging out, I'm working. When I'm hanging out, they're working. My closest friend is Brooke, because she's basically the same age I am, and we like the same things, and we do everything together."

Jeff and Brooke, now married, enjoy a break at the 1996 Daytona 500.

Say What?

Here's what racing people are saying about Jeff Gordon:

"He's a natural talent."

—*Rusty Wallace,*
  1989 Winston Cup champion

"He's a brilliant young driver who brings a new level of excitement to NASCAR racing."

—*John Perez, sportscaster*

"It was hard for the media to be skeptical and critical of him because he was always so polite. People understood right away he was serious about the sport."

—*Bill Armor, former media relations manager*

"Somebody asked me what I'm going to try to do about him. I said I'm going to try to hire him!"

—*Darrell Waltrip,*
car owner and driver

"He has supreme confidence in himself. He knows he has the potential to become the greatest driver ever."

—*Jimmy Johnson, Hendrick*
Motorsports business manager

"Everyone thinks that it all came so easy to him, but he paid his dues when he was a teenager."

—*Ray Glier, syndicated*
racing columnist

"He's one of these people who can make you sick because whatever he tries he's good at!"

—*Brooke, Jeff's wife*

Jeff, at age 17, won his first USAC race, a 30-lap sprint.

Jeff Gordon has lost count of all the races he has won in his life, but most fans put the number at around 600. At every stop on the road to NASCAR stardom, he was the youngest and the best driver in his classification. Jeff's goal is to win seven Winston Cup championships.

Jeff won the Quarter Midget Grand National Championship in 1978 and 1981.

Jeff was named USAC Midget Rookie of the Year in 1989.

Highlights

t the age of 20, Jeff became the youngest winner of the USAC Championship Dirt Track Title in 1991.

Jeff was named Busch Series Rookie of the Year in 1991.

Jeff wins a 1990 race in Indiana on his way to the USAC National Midget title.

Jeff broke a Busch Series record by recording the highest qualifying speed in 11 events.

Jeff was named Winston Cup Rookie of the Year in 1993.

Jeff won the inaugural running of the Brickyard 400 in 1994.

Jeff won the prestigious Busch Clash to start the 1994 season.

Jeff recorded the fastest qualifying time for the 1995 Brickyard.

Jeff's first win of the 1996 season came at the Pontiac 400 in Virginia.

RICHMOND USA

RIR

AUTOMOTIVE FINISHES

DUPONT

Q Quaker State

24

GMAC

Jeff's first Winston Cup victory came at the 1994 Coca-Cola 600 in Atlanta.

Jeff became the second-youngest NASCAR champion in history in 1995.

Jeff won his eleventh career race at Darlington, South Carolina, in 1996.

Reaching

Jeff is one of the few top NASCAR drivers who can race clean and fast. He is skilled enough to charge through the pack without having to nudge somebody out of the way.

The hardest thing that Jeff Gordon as a NASCAR superstar has had to learn is how to say no. There are more good causes and needy people out there than he can possibly devote his time and energy to. One organization he always has time for, however, is the Leukemia Society. It is a cause that became very close to his heart when crew chief Ray Evernham's son was diagnosed with the disease in 1992. Once, Jeff chartered a private plane so that he would not miss Ray Jr.'s birthday party. "We have more than just a friendship. His little boy, Ray Jay, is very special to me, as is his whole family."

Jeff became a supporter of the Leukemia Society after the son of crew chief Ray Evernham (left) contracted the disease.

Out

Wherever he goes at the track, Jeff will gladly sign autographs.

Numbers

Name: Jeff Gordon

Born: August 4, 1971

Height: 5' 7"

Weight: 155 pounds

Car Number: 24

Racing Team: Hendrick Motorsports

At 24, Jeff became the second-youngest champion ever in NASCAR's top division when he won the Winston Cup title in 1995. Bill Rexford won the championship in 1950 at the age of 23.

Year	Starts	Wins	2nd	3rd	4th	5th	Prize Money
1992	1	0	0	0	0	0	$ 6,285
1993	30	0	2	1	1	3	$ 765,168
1994	31	2	1	1	2	1	$1,779,523
1995	31	7	4	5	0	1	$2,430,460
Totals	93	9	7	7	3	5	$4,981,436

Glossary

COVETED highly desired

DYNASTY a powerful team that maintains its position for a long time

FORMIDABLE having awesome qualities; unapproachable

INAUGURAL a formal opening or beginning

LEUKEMIA SOCIETY an organization that raises money to fight leukemia, a cancer-related blood disease

PHYSICS a science that deals with mass and energy and how they work together

PINNACLE the highest point of development or achievement

PREMIUM a sum over and above a regular price

PRODIGY a young person with an extraordinary talent

SKEPTICAL full of doubt; critical

VETERAN one who has a lot of experience

Index

About The Author

Mark Stewart grew up in New York City in the 1960s and 1970s– when the Mets, Jets, and Knicks all had championship teams. As a child, Mark read everything about sports he could lay his hands on. Today, he is one of the busiest sportswriters around. Since 1990, he has written close to 500 sports stories for kids, including profiles on more than 200 athletes, past and present. A graduate of Duke University, Mark served as senior editor of *Racquet*, a national tennis magazine, and was managing editor of *Super News*, a sporting goods industry newspaper. He is the author of every Grolier All-Pro Biography.